Explanation of Riyaadh Saliheen:

The Chapter on the Prohibition of Arrogance & Self-Conceit

SHAYKH MUHAMMAD BIN SALEH AL-'UTHAYMEEN

ISBN: 978-1-6289-0608-0

First Edition: Rabee' Awwal 1435 A.H. / January 2014 C.E.

Cover Design: Maktabatulirshad staff
E-mail: Maktabatulirshad@gmail.com

Translation by Aboo Sulaymaan Muhammad 'Abdul-Azim bin Joshua Baker

Revision of Translation by: Aboo Yusuf 'Abdullaah Ibrahim Omran Al-Misri

Editing: Deliberate Ink
E-mail: shakirah@deliberateink.com

Typesetting and Formatting: Aboo Sulaymaan Muhammad 'Abdul-Azim bin Joshua Baker

Subject: Hadeeth

Website: www.maktabatulirshad.webs.com

E-mail: Maktabatulirshad@gmail.com

TABLE OF CONTENTS

BIOGRAPHY OF THE EXPLAINER

Al-Allaamah Muhammad Bin Saleh Al-
'Uthaymeen (1347-1421AH)

His lineage and birth: He is the noble scholar,
verifier, Faqeeh, scholar of Tafsir, god-fearing,
ascetic, Muhammad Bin Saleh Bin Muhammad
bin Sulaymaan bin 'Abd-Rahman Ali
'Uthaymeen from *Al-Wahbah* of Bani Tameem.
He was born on the 27th night of the blessed
month Ramadan in the year 1347AH in
'Unayzah –one of the cities of Al-Qaseem- in the
kingdom of Saudia Arabia.

His scholastic upbringing: his father, may
Allaah have mercy upon him, enrolled him to
study the Noble Quran with his maternal
grandfather, the teacher 'Abdur-Rahman Bin
Sulaymaan Ad-Daamigh', may Allaah have
mercy upon him. Then he studied writing, some
arithmetic, and Arabic literature at *"Al-Ustaadh
'Abdul-Azeez Bin Saleh Ad-Daamigh's school"*;
and that was before he enrolled in *"Al-Mu'allim*

'Ali Bin 'Abdillah Ash-Shahaytan's School" where
he memorized the Noble Quran with him, and he
had not reached fourteen years of age yet.

Under the direction of his father, may Allaah
have mercy upon him, he embarked upon
seeking religious knowledge; and the noble
Shaykh Al-'Allamah 'Abdur Rahman Bin Nasir
As-Sa'dee, may Allâh have mercy upon him, use
to teach religious sciences and Arabic at *"Jaame'*
Kabeer" (i.e. Grand masjid where Jumu'ah his
held) in 'Unayzah. He arranged two of his senior
students to teach the beginning students.
Therefore, the Shaykh (i.e. Al-'Uthaymeen) would
join Shaykh Muhammad Bin 'Abdul-'Azeez Al-
Mutawwa's circle of knowledge, may Allâh have
mercy upon him, until he attained from
knowledge of *Tawheed, Fiqh,* and *Nahw* (i.e.
Arabic grammar related to the ending of words)
what he attained.

Then he sat in the circles of knowledge of his
Shaykh 'Abdur Rahman Bin Nasir As-Sa'dee,
may Allaah have mercy upon him. So he studied
with him Tafsir, Hadith, Seerah of the Prophet,
At-Tawheed, Al-Fiqh, Al-'Usool, Al-Faraa'id, An-

Nahw, and memorization concise texts on these sciences.

The noble Shaykh Al-'Allamah 'Abdur Rahman Bin Nasir As-Sa'dee, May Allaah have mercy upon him, was considered to be his first Shaykh. Since he acquired knowledge, experience, and methods (of learning) from him more so than anyone else; and he was impressed by his methodology, his principles, his way of teaching, and his adherence to proofs and evidences.

When Shaykh 'Abdur-Rahman Bin 'Ali Bin 'Awdaan, may Allaah have mercy upon him, was a judge in 'Unayzah he (i.e. Shaykh Al-'Uthaymeen) would study the science of Al-Faraa'id with him, just like he would study An-Nahw and Al-Balaghah with Shaykh 'Abdur-Razzaaq 'Afeefee, may Allâh have mercy upon him, during his presence as a teacher in that city.

When the academic institution opened in Riyadh, some of his brothers urged him to enroll. So he sought his Shaykh's, 'Abdur Rahman Bin Nasir As-Sa'dee, may Allaah have mercy upon him, permission. So he gave him permission, and he enrolled in the institution from 1372AH to 1373AH.

Indeed he took advantage of the scholars who use to teach there at that time, through the two years that he entered in the academic institution in Riyadh. Among them was Al-'Allamah, scholar in Tafsir Shaykh Muhammad Al-Ameen As-Shanqitee, Shaykh Al-Faqeeh 'Abdul-'Azeez Bin Nasir Bin Rasheed, and Shaykh, the scholar in hadith, 'Abdur-Rahman Al-Ifreekee…may Allaah have mercy upon them.

During that time, he would stick with His eminence Shaykh Al-'Allamah 'Abdul-'Azeez Bin 'Abdillah Bin Baaz, may Allaah have mercy upon him, and he studied with him Saheeh Bukhari and some treatises of Shaykhul-Islam Ibn Taymiyah in the masjid. He benefited by him in the science of hadith, analyzing the views of the scholars of fiqh and the relationship between them. He considered Shaykh 'Abdul-'Azeez Bin Baaz, may Allaah have mercy upon him, to be his second Shaykh in obtaining knowledge and being influenced by him.

Then he returned to 'Unayzah in 1374AH, and he commenced studying under his Shaykh Al-

'Allamah 'Abdur-Rahman Bin Nasir As-Sa'dee and he followed up his studies in the faculty of Sharee'ah, which had become a subsidiary of Imam Muhammad Bin Saud Islamic University until he obtained a high-ranking degree.

His teaching: his Shaykh saw in him nobleness and quickness in the acquisition of knowledge, so he encouraged him to teach while he was still a student in his circles of knowledge. So he began teaching in 1370 at the *"Jaamee Kabeer"* in 'Unayzah.

When he graduated from the institute in Riyadh, he was appointed as a teacher at the institution in 'Unayzah in 1374AH.

In 1376AH, his Shaykh Al-'Allamah 'Abdur-Rahman Bin Nasir as-Sa'dee, may Allaah have mercy upon him, died. Therefore, he (i.e. Al-'Uthaymeen) was appointed the imamate of "Jaamee Kabeer" in 'Unayzah and also he was appointed the imamate of two 'Eid there, and he was appointed to teach in the library of 'Unayzah Al-Wataniyah next to Jaamee Kabeer, which his Shaykh, founded in 1359AH.

When the number of students increased, and the library could not suffice them, the noble Shaykh began teaching in the Masjid Al-Jaamee.

The students gathered there, and they would flock together from Kingdom of Saudia Arabia and outside of the Kingdom until they reached in the hundreds for some of the classes. These people studied seriously, and they did not just simply listened to the classes. He (i.e. 'Uthaymeen) remained upon that as an Imam, a Khateeb, and a teacher until his passing, may Allaah have mercy upon him.

The Shaykh remained a teacher in the institution from 1374AH to 1398AH, and when he transferred to teaching in the faculty of *Sharee'ah* and *Usool-Deen* in Al-Qaseem branch to Muhammad Bin Saud Islamic University and remained as a teacher there until his passing away, May Allaah the most high have mercy upon him.

He use to lecture in *Masjid Haram* and *Masjid An-Nabawi* during the seasons of Hajj, Ramadan, and the summer vacations from 1402AH until his passing away, may Allaah have mercy upon him.

The Shaykh had a particular teaching practice in his openhandedness and integrity. He would raise questions to his students, receive their questions, and hold classes and lectures with a lofty concern, a composed mind and delighted at his propagating religious knowledge and his closeness to the people.

His passing away: He passed away, may Allaah have mercy upon him, in the city of Jeddah shortly before Maghrib on Wednesday the 15th of the month of Shawwal 1421AH. He was prayed over in *Masjid Haram* after 'Asr on Thursday. Then he was followed by thousands who had prayed over him, and he was buried in *Mecca Al-Mukaramah.* [1]

---

[1] The source of this is biography was from the Shaykh's website (www.ibnothaimeen.com)

CHAPTER 72

THE PROHIBITION OF ARROGANCE AND SELF-CONCEIT

Allaah The Sublime says,

﴿ تِلْكَ ٱلدَّارُ ٱلْأَخِرَةُ نَجْعَلُهَا لِلَّذِينَ لَا يُرِيدُونَ عُلُوًّا فِى ٱلْأَرْضِ وَلَا
فَسَادًا وَٱلْعَٰقِبَةُ لِلْمُتَّقِينَ ﴿٨٣﴾ ﴾

"That home of the Hereafter (i.e. Paradise), We shall assign to those who rebel not against the truth with pride and oppression in the land nor do mischief by committing crimes. And the good end is for the *Muttaqûn* (pious)." [2]

And Allaah the Sublime says,

﴿ وَلَا تَمْشِ فِى ٱلْأَرْضِ مَرَحًا إِنَّكَ لَن تَخْرِقَ ٱلْأَرْضَ وَلَن تَبْلُغَ ٱلْجِبَالَ
طُولًا ﴿٣٧﴾ ﴾

"And walk not on the earth with conceit and arrogance. Verily, you can neither

---

[2] Al-Qasas (28:83)

split nor penetrate the earth, nor can you attain a stature like the mountains in height." [3]

And Allaah, the Sublime says,

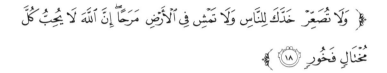

"And turn not your face away from men with pride, nor walk in insolence through the earth. Verily, Allaah likes not any arrogant boaster." [4]

The meaning behind the statement, **"And turn not your face away from men with pride"** is that you turn your attention away from the people and reject them out of arrogance; and the word **"pride"** refers to swaggering.

And Allaah the Sublime says,

﴿ ۞ إِنَّ قَـٰرُونَ كَانَ مِن قَوْمِ مُوسَىٰ فَبَغَىٰ عَلَيْهِمْ وَءَاتَيْنَـٰهُ مِنَ
ٱلْكُنُوزِ مَآ إِنَّ مَفَاتِحَهُۥ لَتَنُوٓأُ بِٱلْعُصْبَةِ أُوْلِى ٱلْقُوَّةِ إِذْ قَالَ لَهُۥ قَوْمُهُۥ لَا
تَفْرَحْ إِنَّ ٱللَّهَ لَا يُحِبُّ ٱلْفَرِحِينَ ﴿٧٦﴾ ﴾

---

[3] Al-Isra' (17:37)
[4] Luqman (31:18)

"Verily, Qaarun (Korah) was of Mûsa's (Moses) people, but he behaved arrogantly towards them. And We gave him of the treasures, the keys of which would have been a burden to a group of strong men. When his people said to him: "Do not be proud (with ungratefulness to Allaah's Favours). Verily! Allaah likes not those who are proud (with ungratefulness to Allaah's Favours)." [5]

Up until Allaah the Sublime says,[6]

---

[5] Al-Qasas (28:76)

[6] **Translator's note:** the following verses are mentioned between what the author has cited: **"But seek, with that (wealth) which Allaah has bestowed on you, the home of the Hereafter, and forget not your portion of legal enjoyment in this world, and do good as Allaah has been good to you, and seek not mischief in the land. Verily, Allaah likes not the *Mufsidûn* (those who commit great crimes and sins, oppressors, tyrants, mischief-makers, corrupt). He says: "This has been given to me only because of knowledge I possess." Did he not know that Allaah had destroyed before him generations of men who were stronger than him in might and greater in the amount (of riches) than they had collected. But the *Mujrimûn* (criminals, disbelievers, polytheists, sinners, etc.) will not be questioned of their sins (because Allaah knows them well, so they will be punished without account). So he went forth before his people in his pomp. Those who were desirous of the life of the world, said: "Ah, would**

﴿ فَخَسَفْنَا بِهِۦ وَبِدَارِهِ ٱلْأَرْضَ ﴾

**"So We caused the earth to swallow him
and his dwelling place."** [7]

Explanation

The author, An-Nawawi (*rahimahullah*) said in
his book *Riyadh As-Saliheen* concerning what he
cited of arrogance and self-conceit:

Arrogance: A belief in one's own greatness above
the people, and possession of virtue over them.

Self-conceit: Looking at one's actions and
becoming amazed by them; regarding them as
great and lofty.

So self-conceit describes one's actions while
arrogance describes one's soul. Both traits are
dispraised.

---

that we had the like of what Qaarun (Korah) has been
given. Verily! He is the owner of a great fortune." But
those who had been given (religious) knowledge said:
"Woe to you! The Reward of Allaah (in the Hereafter) is
better for those who believe and do righteous good
deeds, and this none shall attain except those who are
patient (in following the truth)." Al-Qasas (28:77-80)
[7] Al-Qasas (28:81)

Arrogance is of two types: Arrogance toward the truth and arrogance toward people. The Prophet (*sallallahu 'alayhi wa sallam*) clarified both in his statement,

الْكِبَرُ بَطَرُ الْحَقِّ وَ غَمْطُ النَّاسِ

"Arrogance is to reject the truth and to belittle the people."[8]

The meaning behind the statement, **"reject the truth"** is to discard it, be averse to it, and to deny it; and the meaning behind the statement, **"belittle the people"** is to disparage and disdain them, and deem people to be of no worth, seeing oneself above them.

It was said to one man, "What do you think of the people?" He said, "I don't view them in any way except as flies." So it is said to him, "Indeed they don't think of you in any way except the same."

And it was said to another, "What do you think of the people?" He said, "I view the people to be greater than me; that they have a position and status." So it was said to him, "Indeed they view

---

[8] Muslim collected it in Kitaabul Emaan under the chapter **"The prohibition of arrogance and its clarification"** (91).

you to be greater than them, and that you have a position and status." When one views people in a certain way, people view one likewise. If one views them with honor, respect, and admiration, placing them in their rightful status, they will hold one in high esteem and will view one in a position of respect, veneration, and great importance, placing one in one's rightful position, and vice versa.

The Prophet's *(sallallahu 'alayhi wa sallam)* statement, **"reject the truth"** means discarding the truth and not accepting it; because of thinking highly of oneself and one's opinion. He views himself greater than the truth, Allaah forbid. The sign of such is that evidences from the Book and Sunnah are brought before him yet he will not accept them; instead persisting in his stubbornness. This is the exact description of rejecting the truth, Allaah forbid.

Many people are relentless in supporting their own positions. When they make a statement, they won't budge even if it opposes the truth. The obligation is that the person returns to the truth wherever he discovers it even if contradicts his statement. Indeed, this is more honorable before Allaah and the people; this clears his name and brings no harm.

Thus, one should not assume that if one retracts one's statement, one's position will be debased before the people. On the contrary, this will raise one's position and the people will know that one adheres only to the truth. As for the one who is persistent in wrongful statements and discards the truth, this is arrogance, Allaah forbid.

This second (matter) happens to some people, including the students of knowledge, Allaah forbid. Some of them deny the truth after a discussion that proved their position invalid. In fact, Shaytaan whispers to him that if he recants his view, people will undervalue him saying, "This is a weak-minded person whose opinions are constantly changeable." But this will not harm him if he returns to the truth. Hence it's of no harm to have various positions. The honorable Imams had numerous statements for one issue.

Here is Imam Ahmad *(rahimahullah)*, the Imam of Ahlus-Sunnah—the greatest of Imams regarding vast knowledge and adherence to textual evidence. We find that at times he held four statements regarding one matter. Why is that? Because when a new proof appeared to him, he changed his view accordingly. This should be the way of every righteous person: to be obliged to adhere to the proofs, wherever they may be.

The author (*rahimahullah*) cited the verse related to this chapter, clarifying that every verse mentioned proves the dispraise of arrogance; and the last verses are related to Qaaroon. He was a man from the children of Isra'il; from Musa's people. Allaah, The Glorified and Sublime, had bestowed upon Qaaroon abundant wealth; so much that its keys were too heavy to be carried by a strong group.

$$﴿ إِذْ قَالَ لَهُۥ قَوْمُهُۥ لَا تَفْرَحْ إِنَّ ٱللَّهَ لَا يُحِبُّ ٱلْفَرِحِينَ ۝ ﴾$$

"When his people said to him: "Do not be proud (with ungratefulness to Allaah's Favours). Verily! Allaah likes not those who are proud (with ungratefulness to Allaah's Favours)." [9]

This man had hubris and arrogance, Allaah forbid. When he was reminded of Allaah's signs, he denied them and was arrogant. He said,

$$﴿ قَالَ إِنَّمَآ أُوتِيتُهُۥ عَلَىٰ عِلْمٍ عِندِىٓ ﴾$$

---

[9] Al-Qasas (28:76)

"This has been given to me only because of knowledge I possess." [10]

Then he denied Allaah's favors upon him saying,

﴿ قَالَ إِنَّمَآ أُوتِيتُهُۥ عَلَىٰ عِلْمٍ عِندِىٓ ﴾

"I acquired this wealth through my own efforts and knowledge."

Consequently, Allaah caused the earth to swallow him and his house after the deaths of his viceroys and himself.

﴿ فَمَا كَانَ لَهُۥ مِن فِئَةٍ يَنصُرُونَهُۥ مِن دُونِ ٱللَّهِ وَمَا كَانَ مِنَ ٱلْمُنتَصِرِينَ ۝ وَأَصْبَحَ ٱلَّذِينَ تَمَنَّوْا۟ مَكَانَهُۥ بِٱلْأَمْسِ يَقُولُونَ وَيْكَأَنَّ ٱللَّهَ يَبْسُطُ ٱلرِّزْقَ لِمَن يَشَآءُ مِنْ عِبَادِهِۦ وَيَقْدِرُ لَوْلَآ أَن مَّنَّ ٱللَّهُ عَلَيْنَا لَخَسَفَ بِنَا ﴾

"Then he had no group or party to help him against Allaah, nor was he one of those who could save themselves. And those who had desired (for a position like) his position the day before, began to say: "Know not that it is Allaah

---

Who enlarges the provision or restricts it to whomsoever He pleases of His slaves? Had it not been that Allaah was gracious to us, He could have caused the earth to swallow us up (also)!" [11]

Contemplate on the consequences of arrogance, self-conceit, and boasting about oneself—Allaah forbid—and their yield of death and destruction.

Afterward, the author cites a number of verses, among them His statement, the Sublime:

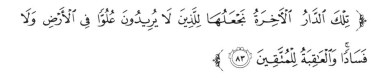

"That home of the Hereafter (i.e. Paradise), We shall assign to those who rebel not against the truth with pride and oppression in the land nor do mischief by committing crimes. And the good end is for the *Muttaqûn*." [12]

The Hereafter is the final abode for the children of Aadam, since they have four abodes, which eventually lead to the Hereafter. The first abode is the womb of the mother. The second abode is

---

[11] Al-Qasas (28:81-82)
[12] Al-Qasas (28:83)

the transitional period after leaving the mother's womb to enter the world.

The third abode is the grave, which is between death and the establishment of the last hour. The fourth abode is the final abode, which is the last and eternal abode. Allaah the Sublime says about this abode,

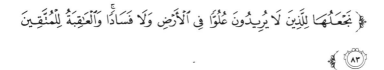

"We shall assign (Paradise) to those who rebel not against the truth with pride and oppression in the land nor do mischief." [13]

Those referred to in the verse do not yearn for rebellion against the truth, nor against their fellow peoples; instead they are humble. Allaah hasn't described them with the desire for haughtiness and corruption. People are categorized into three groups:

1. A group that is haughty, corrupt, and cause corruption; this group produces and inflicts corruption.

---

[13] Al-Qasas (28:83)

2. A group that doesn't desire corruption nor haughtiness; this group neither produce nor inflict any harm.

3. A group that desires haughtiness and corruption; nevertheless it is unable to initiate it.

This third group takes a middle course between the first two groups; nonetheless, they are sinners since they desired evil. On the other hand, the abode of the hereafter is only for "those who rebel not against the truth with pride and oppression in the land." Meaning those who neither display any sign of superiority over people nor over the truth.

"...nor do mischief by committing crimes. And the good end is for the Muttaqûn".

One may ask, "What is the meaning behind Allaah's statement, "mischief throughout the earth?" The answer is that "mischief throughout the earth" doesn't refer to the destruction of homes and burning of farms; on the contrary, it refers to acts of disobedience, as the people of knowledge (*rahimahumallah*) commented regarding Allaah's statement,

$$\lbrace\ \text{وَلَا تُفْسِدُواْ فِى ٱلْأَرْضِ بَعْدَ إِصْلَٰحِهَا}\ \rbrace$$

"And do not do mischief on the earth, after it has been set in order." [14]

Meaning, do not be disobedient to Allaah as it results in mischief. Allaah, the Blessed and Sublime says,

$$\lbrace\ \text{وَلَوْ أَنَّ أَهْلَ ٱلْقُرَىٰٓ ءَامَنُواْ وَٱتَّقَوْاْ لَفَتَحْنَا عَلَيْهِم بَرَكَٰتٍ مِّنَ ٱلسَّمَآءِ}$$
$$\text{وَٱلْأَرْضِ وَلَٰكِن كَذَّبُواْ فَأَخَذْنَٰهُم بِمَا كَانُواْ يَكْسِبُونَ}\ \text{(٩٦)}\ \rbrace$$

"And if the people of the towns had believed and had *taqwâ* (piety), certainly, We should have opened for them blessings from the heaven and the earth, but they belied (the Messengers). So We took them (with punishment) for what they used to earn." [15]

Allaah did not open for them blessings from the heavens and earth. The mischief throughout the

---

[14] Al-'Araaf (7:56)
[15] Al-'Araaf (7:96)

earth was because of their disobedience, and we ask Allaah for safety.

Allaah the Blessed and Sublime says,

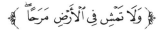

"... nor walk in insolence through the earth." [16]

Meaning do not walk boastfully and arrogantly. In the second verse the author mentioned what Allaah says,

"Verily, you can neither rend nor penetrate the earth, nor can you attain a stature like the mountains in height." [17]

Meaning, no matter who one is, one will not be able to rend the earth and boast even if one were on the same level as the mountain. One is who one is: a son of Aadam, insignificant and weak. How can one walk in insolence through the earth?

Allaah the Sublime says,

---

[16] Luqman (31:18)
[17] Al-Isra (17:37)

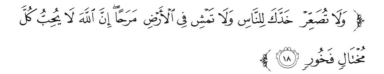

"And turn not your face away from men with pride, nor walk in insolence through the earth. Verily, Allaah likes not any arrogant boaster."

The meaning behind **"turning your face away from men with pride"** refers to rejection of people. Such people are, Allaah forbid, arrogant. Those people tend to disdain others' talks and turn away from listening to them.

The meaning behind **"nor walk in insolence through the earth"** is not to walk with arrogance and self-conceit.

The meaning behind **"Verily, Allaah likes not any arrogant boaster"** refers to a person who is arrogant in appearance and boastful in speech. He is arrogant in his appearance, in his clothing and his walking. Allaah the Sublime does not like such behavior; rather, Allaah likes the humble person who keeps his status hidden from the people and who has *taqwaa*.

This is what Allaah, the Mighty and Sublime, likes. We ask Allaah, the Sublime, to guide us all to the best manners and actions; and to keep us distant from evil manners and deeds. Indeed He is Openhanded and Most Generous.

HADITH NUMBER 612 & 613

(١) ٦١٢ - وَ عَنْ عَبْدِ الله بْنِ مَسْعُودٍ رَضِيَ اللهُ عَنْهُ، عَنِ النَّبِيِّ صَلَّى اللهُ عَلَيْهِ وَ سَلَّمَ قَالَ : ((لَا يَدْخُلُ الْجَنَّةَ مَنْ كَانَ فِي قَلْبِهِ مِثْقَالُ ذَرَّةٍ مِنْ كِبْرٍ)) فَقَالَ رَجُلٌ : إِنَّ الرَّجُلَ يُحِبُّ أَنْ يَكُونَ ثَوْبُهُ حَسَنًا، وَ نَعْلُهُ حَسَنَةً ؟ قَالَ : ((إِنَّ اللهَ جَمِيلٌ يُحِبُّ الْجِمَالَ . الْكِبْرُ بَطَرُ الْحَقِّ وَ غَمْطُ النَّاسِ)) رَوَاهُ مُسْلِمٌ .

((بَطَرُ الْحَقِّ)) : دَفْعُهُ وَ رَدُّهُ عَلَى قَائِلِهِ . ((وَ غَمْطُ النَّاسِ)) : اِحْتِقَارُهُمْ .

1/612- On the authority of 'Abdillah bin Mas'ood (*radhiallahu 'anhu*), the Prophet (*sallallahu 'alayhi wa sallam*) said, "No one will enter Paradise who has an atom's weight of arrogance within his heart." So a man said, "Is this the man who loves to have beautiful clothes and shoes?" The Prophet said, "Indeed Allaah is *Jameel* and He loves

beauty; however, arrogance is to reject the truth and belittle the people.” Muslim collected it. [18]

The statement, **“reject the truth”** refers to rebutting and refusing the one saying it (the truth) while the statement, **“belittle the people”** refers to scorning them.

(٢) ٦١٣- وَ عَنْ سَلَمَةَ بْنِ الْأَكْوَعِ رَضِيَ اللهُ عَنْهُ أَنَّ رَجُلاً أَكَلَ عِنْدَ رَسُولِ اللهِ صَلَّى اللهُ عَلَيْهِ وَ سَلَّمَ بِشِمَالِهِ، فَقَالَ: ((كُلْ بِيَمِينِكَ)). قَالَ: لَا أَسْتَطِيعُ! قَالَ: ((لَا اسْتَطَعْتَ)) مَا مَنَعَهُ إِلَّا الْكِبْرُ. قَالَ: فَمَا رَفَعَهَا إِلَى فِيهِ. رَوَاهُ مُسْلِمٌ

2/613- And on the authority of Salamah bin Al-Akwaa’ (*radhiallahu ‘anhu*), a man was eating with his left hand in the company of Allaah’s Messenger (*sallallahu ‘alayhi wa sallam*) so the Prophet (*sallallahu ‘alayhi wa sallam*) said, “Eat with your right hand.” The man said, “I can’t!” So the Prophet (*sallallahu ‘alayhi wa sallam*) said to him,

---

[18] Muslim collected it in Kitaabul Emaan under the chapter **“The prohibition of arrogance and a clarification of it”** (91).

"Would that you will never be able to."
Nothing deterred this man (from obeying)
except arrogance. He (the narrator) said, "So
he wasn't able to raise his right hand to his
mouth after that." Muslim collected it [19]

Explanation

The author, An-Nawawi (*rahimahullah*) said in
his book *Riyadh As-Saliheen* under the chapter
"The prohibition of arrogance and self-conceit"
from the hadith of 'Abdullaah bin Mas'ood
(*radhiallahu 'anhu*) that the Prophet (*sallallahu
'alayhi wa sallam*) said,

$$لَا يَدْخُلُ الْـجَنَّةَ مَـنْ كَانَ فِي قَلْبِهِ مِثْقَالُ ذَرَّةٍ$$

$$مِنْ كِبْرٍ$$

**"No one will enter Paradise who has an
atom's weight of arrogance within his
heart."**

This hadith is classified under the warning
category, which the Prophet (*sallallahu 'alayhi*

---

[19] Muslim collected it in Kitaabul Ashribah under the
chapter **"Etiquettes concerning food and drink"** (2021)

wa sallam) employed to drive people away from danger, although (these hadith) require detailed explanation consistent with the textual evidence.

As for the one who has arrogance in one's heart, this arrogance can be manifested in one's rejection of the truth and harboring hatred towards it. This is disbelief that will send one to Hell for eternity, never to enter Paradise, because of Allaah's statement,

$$ ﴾ ۝ ذَٰلِكَ بِأَنَّهُمْ كَرِهُوا۟ مَآ أَنزَلَ ٱللَّهُ فَأَحْبَطَ أَعْمَٰلَهُمْ ﴿ $$

"That is because they hate that which Allaah has sent down (this Qur'ân and Islâmic laws, etc.), so He has made their deeds fruitless." [20]

Their deeds were not rendered fruitless for any reason except disbelief, just as Allaah the Sublime says,

$$ ﴾ وَمَن يَرْتَدِدْ مِنكُمْ عَن دِينِهِۦ فَيَمُتْ وَهُوَ كَافِرٌ فَأُو۟لَٰٓئِكَ حَبِطَتْ أَعْمَٰلُهُمْ فِى ٱلدُّنْيَا وَٱلْءَاخِرَةِ وَأُو۟لَٰٓئِكَ أَصْحَٰبُ ٱلنَّارِ هُمْ فِيهَا خَٰلِدُونَ ۝ ﴿ $$

"And whosoever of you turns back from his religion and dies as a disbeliever,

---

[20] Muhammad (47:9)

then his deeds will be lost in this life and in the Hereafter, and they will be the dwellers of the Fire. They will abide therein forever." [21]

Arrogance could also be in believing to be more superior than people; yet he doesn't have the same attitude concerning the worship of Allah. This person will not enter Paradise without being punished first. It is imperative that he be punished in return for his unbearable arrogance. Afterwards, he shall enter Paradise after he has been completely purified.

When the Prophet (*sallallahu 'alayhi wa sallam*) narrated this hadith, a man asked him,

يَا رَسُولَ الله الرَّجُلَ يُحِبُّ أَنْ يَكُونَ ثَوْبُهُ حَسَنًا

وَ نَعْلُهُ حَسَنَةً؟

"O Allaah's Messenger, is that the man who loves to have beautiful clothes and shoes?"

Meaning: is this desire one of arrogance? And the Prophet (*sallallahu 'alayhi wa sallam*) said,

---

[21] Al-Baqarah (2:217)

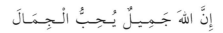

إِنَّ اللهَ جَمِيلٌ يُحِبُّ الْجِمَالَ

"Indeed Allaah is *Jameel* and He loves beauty."

This beauty refers to Allaah's Self, actions, and attributes. All of what originates from Allaah, the Mighty and Sublime is *Jameel* and is not repugnant. Rather it is superb, met with pleasure and acceptance by sound-minded individuals.

The Prophet's statement **"He loves beauty"** asserts that Allaah loves beautification; Allaah asserts that one should beautify his clothes, shoes, body, and in all of his affairs since beautification attracts the peoples' hearts to that individual and draws their admiration, in contrast to ugliness of the hair, shirt, or clothes.

So the Prophet (*sallallahu 'alayhi wa sallam*) said,

إِنَّ اللهَ جَمِيلٌ يُحِبُّ الْجِمَالَ

"Indeed Allaah is *Jameel* and He loves beauty,"

Meaning, He loves that a person beautifies himself. As for the beauty of one's physical appearance/complexion, which Allaah, the

Mighty and Sublime bestows, this is solely up to
Allaah, the Glorified and Sublime. The person is
helpless in respect to this matter. The hadith
highlights what the person does have control
over in terms of beautifying oneself.

As for the second hadith, the hadith of Salamah
bin Al-Akwaa' (*radhiallahu 'anhu*) in which a
man was eating with his left hand in the
company of the Prophet (*sallallahu 'alayhi wa
sallam*) and he said,

كُلْ بِيَمِينِكَ

"Eat with your right hand."

The man replied, **"I am not able"** and nothing
deterred him except arrogance.

So the Prophet *(sallallahu 'alayhi wa sallam)*
said,

لَا اسْتَطَعْتَ

"Would that you will never be able to,"

Meaning the Prophet *(sallallahu 'alayhi wa
sallam)* supplicated to Allaah the Sublime to
strike the man in a manner that would disable
him from raising his hand to his mouth after

that. As a consequence, Allaah forbid, his hand was rendered useless as a stick and he was no longer able to raise it because of his arrogance to the religion of Allaah, the Mighty and Sublime.

This hadith alludes to the obligation of eating and drinking with the right hand. Eating with the left hand is unlawful and considered a sin. Likewise, drinking with the left hand has the same verdict. Eating and drinking with the left hand resembles Shaytan and his allies. The Prophet (*sallallahu 'alayhi wa sallam*) said,

لَا يَأْكُلْ أَحَدُكُمْ بِشِمَالِهِ وَ لَا يَشْرَبُ بِشِمَالِهِ

فَإِنَّ الشَّيْطَانَ يَأْكُلُ بِشِمَالِهِ وَ يَشْرَبُ بِشِمَالِهِ .

"None of you should eat or drink with his left hand because verily Shaytan eats and drinks with his left hand."[22]

When we look at the disbelievers today, we notice them eating and drinking with their left hand; doing as they do is deemed an imitation of the Shaytan and his allies. Nevertheless, correction must be made in the most excellent manner, by being subtle if one fears that the person being corrected will become embarrassed, scornful and arrogant. One should

---

[22] Muslim collected it in Kitaabul Ash'ribah under the chapter **"Etiquettes concerning food and drink"** (2020).

say, "Among the people are those who eat or drink with their left hand, and this is unlawful and impermissible." If one is with a student of knowledge, instruct him in the form of a question, by asking, "What do you say regarding the person who eats and drinks with his left hand?" in order to alert him. So if the person takes heed then this is what is desired, otherwise it should be said to him—in secret if necessary, "Don't eat or drink with your left hand," in order for him to learn the religion and legislation of Allaah, the Sublime.

There are some wealthy people who eat and drink with their right hand except when they drink and eat at the same time. Then they drink with their left hand, claiming if they drink with the right (while eating with the right) the cup will become dirty. It should be said to someone like this, "The matter of either eating or drinking with the left hand is not to be held as insignificant or just undesirable." That gives one the right to instruct that doing so is an act of disobedience because it is unlawful, and unlawful matters are not permissible except in a crisis, and there is no crisis in drinking with the left hand fearing dirtying the cup with food.

Afterwards, it is possible the cup can become dirty so it is feasible that he can grab the cup with his thumb and index finger from the bottom so it doesn't get dirty. This matter will be made easy for whoever wants good and the truth; but as for the stubborn person, the wealthy, or those who blindly follow Allaah's enemies among the Shaytan and his allies this is a (difficult) matter, and Allaah is the One who grants success.

HADITH NUMBERS 614, 615, & 616

(٣) ٦١٤ – وَ عَنْ حَارِثَةَ بْنِ وَهْبٍ رَضِيَ اللهُ عَنْهُ قَالَ :
سَمِعْتُ رَسُولَ الله صَلَّى اللهُ عَلَيْهِ وَ سَلَّمَ يَقُولُ : ((أَلَا
أُخْبِرُكُمْ بِأَهْلِ النَّارِ)) : كُلُّ عُتُلٍّ جَوَّاظٍ مُسْتَكْبِرٍ .
مُتَّفَقٌ عَلَيْهِ . وَ تَقَدَّمَ شَرْحُهُ فِي بَابِ ضَعْفَةِ
الْمُسْلِمِينَ .

3/614- On the authority of Harith bin Wahb (*radhiallahu 'anhu*) he said, "I heard Allaah's Messenger (*sallallahu 'alayhi wa sallam*) saying, "Shall I not tell you about the people of Hell? It is every hardhearted, swaggerer, and arrogant person." (Agreed upon)[23]

This hadith is explained in the chapter "The weakness of the Muslims."

---

[23] Al-Bukhari collected it in Kitaabul Tafseer under the chapter **"Cruel, after all that base-born (of illegitimate birth)" Surah Qalam (68:13)"** (4918); and Muslim collected it in Kitaabul Jannah under the chapter **"The hellfire which the tyrants will enter and Paradise which..."** (2853).

(٤) ٦١٥- وَ عَنْ أَبِي سَعِيدٍ الْخُدْرِيِّ رَضِيَ اللهُ عَنْهُ،
عَنِ النَّبِيِّ صَلَّى اللهُ عَلَيْهِ وَ سَلَّمَ قَالَ : ((احْتَجَّتِ
الْجَنَّةُ وَ النَّارُ، فَقَالَتِ النَّارُ : فِيَّ الْجَبَّارُونَ وَ
الْمُتَكَبِّرُونَ، وَ قَالَتِ الْجَنَّةُ : فِيَّ ضُعَفَاءُ النَّاسِ وَ
مَسَاكِينُهُمْ . فَقَضَى اللهُ بَيْنَهُمَا : إِنَّكِ الْجَنَّةُ
رَحْمَتِي، أَرْحَمُ بِكِ مِنْ أَشَاءُ، وَ إِنَّكِ النَّارُ عَذَابِي،
أُعَذِّبُ بِكِ مَنْ أَشَاءُ، وَ لَكِلَيْكُمَا عَلَيَّ مِلْؤُهَا)) رَوَاهُ
مُسْلِمٌ .

4/615- On the authority of Aboo Sa'eed Al-Khudri (*radhiallahu 'anhu*), the Prophet (*sallallahu 'alayhi wa sallam*) said, "Hell and Paradise were arguing with one another. Hell said, 'my inhabitants are tyrants and the haughty' and Paradise said, 'my inhabitants are the weak and the poor (among the people). So Allaah judged between them. He said, "Indeed you, Paradise, are My Mercy, which I give to whomever I will; and indeed you, Hell, are My Punishment, which I torment whomever I will. It is upon Me to fill

you both up (with inhabitants)." Muslim collected it.[24]

(٥) ٦١٦ - وَ عَنْ أَبِي هُرَيْرَةَ رَضِيَ اللهُ عَـنْـهُ أَنَّ رَسُـولَ اللهِ صَـلَّى اللهُ عَـلَيْهِ وَ سَـلَّـمَ قَالَ : ((لَا يَـنْظُرُ اللهُ يَـوْمَ الْـقِيَـامَةِ إِلَى مَنْ جَرَّ إِزَارَهُ بَـطَرًا)) مُـتَّفَقٌ عَـلَيْهِ .

5/616- On the authority of Aboo Hurairah (*radhiallahu ‘anhu*), Allaah's Messenger (*sallallahu ‘alayhi wa sallam*) said, "Allaah will not look at on the day of resurrection whomever drags his izaar in a vain manner." (Agreed upon.)[25]

Explanation

The author, An-Nawawi (*rahimahullah*), relates these narrations in the book *'Riyaadh As-Saliheen'* under the chapter "The prohibition of arrogance and self-conceit," and we had spoken

---

[24] Muslim collected it in Kitaabul Jannah under the chapter **"The hellfire which the tyrants will enter and Paradise...."** (2847).

[25] Al-Bukhari collected it in Kitaabul Libaas under the chapter **"Whoever among the arrogant drags his thawb"** (5788); and Muslim collected it in Kitaabul Libaas wa Zinaa under the chapter **"The prohibition of dragging the thawb..."** (2087).

about the verses cited in this chapter. Likewise, we had spoken about the narrations the author (*rahimahullah*) mentioned in this chapter.

The author (*rahimahullah*) cited that the Prophet (*sallallahu 'alayhi wa sallam*) said,

أَلَا أُخْبِرُكُمْ بِأَهْلِ النَّارِ

"Shall I not tell you about the people of Hell?"

This rhetorical style the Prophet uses to draw attention to his addresses. When the Prophet (*sallallahu 'alayhi wa sallam*) said,

أَلَا أُخْبِرُكُمْ

"Shall I not tell you?"

Everyone will say, "Yes, inform us O Messenger of Allaah."

He said,

كُلُّ عُتُلٍّ جَوَّاظٍ مُسْتَكْبِرٍ

"It is every hardhearted, swaggerer, and arrogant person."

The word **"hardhearted"** refers to harshness.

The word **"swaggerer"** refers to a person who is loaded with poor traits.

The phrase **"arrogant person"** is our focus in this hadith. It refers to the person who believes himself to be above the truth and people. He will never be softened by the truth nor will he be merciful to the creation, Allaah forbid. These individuals are the inhabitants of Hell.

As for the inhabitants of Paradise, they are weak, poor people who do not have what brings about arrogance; rather, they are always humble without any arrogance or roughness since sometimes wealth corrupts its possessors and encourages them to be arrogant towards the creation and reject the truth, just as Allaah, the Sublime says,

"Nay! Verily, man does transgress all bounds (in disbelief and evil deed, etc.) because he considers himself self-sufficient."[26]

---

[26] Al-'Alaq (96:6-7)

In the same fashion, the hadith concerning the argument between Hell and Paradise, when Hell said,

فِيَّ الْـجَبَّـارُونَ وَ الْـمُتَكَبِّـرُونَ

"Indeed my inhabitants are tyrants and arrogant people,"

and Paradise said,

فِيَّ ضُعَفَاءُ النَّـاسِ وَ مَسَـاكِينُـهُـمْ . فَقَضَى اللهُ بَيْنَهُـمَـا : إِنَّكِ الْـجَنَّةُ رَحْـمَـتِي ، أَرْحَمُ بِـكِ مِنْ أَشَـاءُ ، وَ إِنَّـكِ النَّـارُ عَـذَابِي ، أُعَذِّبُ بِكِ مَـنْ أَشَـاءُ

"Indeed my inhabitants are weak and poor people." So Allaah, the Mighty and Majestic judged between them and said about Paradise, "Indeed you, Paradise, are My Mercy, which I give to whomever I will" and He said to hell, "indeed you, Hell, are My Punishment, which I torment whomever I will."

Thus, Hell was the abode of punishment—Allaah forbid—and Paradise was the abode of mercy; Paradise is Allaah's mercy and the merciful among His servants will dwell in it just as the Prophet (*sallallahu 'alayhi wa sallam*) said,

وَ إِنَّمَا يَرْحَمُ اللهُ مِنْ عِبَادِهِ الرُّحَمَاءَ

"Allaah only shows true mercy to the merciful among His servants." [27]

Allaah then said,

وَ لَكِلَيْكُمَا عَلَيَّ مِلْؤُهَا

"It is upon me to fill you both up (with inhabitants)."

Allaah, the Mighty and Majestic promised to fill Hell and Paradise with inhabitants, and He, the Mighty and Majestic does not break His promise.

Nonetheless, the final outcome will be just as what is authentically narrated and established by the Prophet who maintained that hell will continue to have people entering it and still it will say,

هَلْ مِنْ مَزِيدٍ ؟

"Are there any more?"

---

[27] Al-Bukhari collected it in Kitaabul Janaa'iz under the chapter **"the Prophet's (sallallahu 'alayhi wa sallam) statement, 'he will punish....."** (1284); and Muslim collected it in Kitaabul Janaa'iz under the chapter **"crying for the deceased"** (923).

As Allaah, the Sublime says,

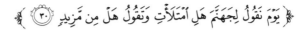

$$﴿ يَوْمَ نَقُولُ لِجَهَنَّمَ هَلِ امْتَلَأْتِ وَتَقُولُ هَلْ مِن مَّزِيدٍ ۝ ﴾$$

"On the Day when We will say to Hell: "Are you filled?" It will say: "Are there any more (to come)?"[28]

Meaning Hell will be demanding more since it has not been filled yet. So the Lord, the Mighty and Majestic will place His Foot on Hell and cause it to close in on itself; and Hell will say,

$$قَطْ قَطْ$$

"Enough, enough."[29]

Meaning, please, enough, enough I don't want any more inhabitants. Thus Hell will become full in this manner.

As for Paradise, indeed Paradise is as Allaah says,

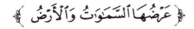

$$﴿ عَرْضُهَا السَّمَوَاتُ وَالْأَرْضُ ﴾$$

---

[28] Qaf (50:30)
[29] Al-Bukhari collected it in Kitaabul Tafseer under the chapter **"Allaah's statement: "Are there any more (to come)?"** (4850); and Muslim collected it in Kitaabul Jannah under the chapter **"the hellfire which the tyrants will enter and Paradise...."** (2846) [36].

"as wide as are the heavens and the earth."[30]

The allies of Allaah will dwell therein. May Allaah make us and you all among them. Its inhabitants will dwell and a surplus will remain, meaning there will be a place where no one will inhabit, so Allaah will bring forth a people whom He will enter into Paradise by His mercy.

The result is that Hell will be filled by the justice of Allaah the Mighty and Majestic, and Paradise will be filled by the virtue and mercy of Allaah the Sublime.

Afterwards, the author (*rahimahullah*) cited a hadith regarding the person who is *musbil* (i.e., one whose clothing drags below his ankles). The Prophet (*'alayhi salaatu wa salaam*) said,

لَا يَنْظُرُ اللهُ يَوْمَ الْقِيَامَةِ إِلَى مَنْ جَرَّ إِزَارَهُ خُيَلَاءَ

"Allaah will not look at on the day of resurrection whomever drags his thawb in a vain manner."

This is a dangerous matter. Men are prohibited from lowering the thawb, pants, or izaar below the ankles. It must be worn slightly above the

---

[30] Aali Imran (3:133)

ankles. Whoever lowers it below the ankles has committed one of the major sins, Allaah forbid.

If he lowers it out of arrogance and self-conceit, Allaah will not look at him on the day of resurrection, nor speak, nor purify him, and the person will have a painful torment. If he lowers it for another reason, for example if it was too long and he did not shorten it, then indeed it has been established from the Prophet (*sallallahu 'alayhi wa sallam*) that he said,

مَا أَسْفَلُ مِنَ الْكَعْبَيْنِ مِنَ الْإِزَارِ فَفِي النَّارِ

"Whatever hangs below the ankles from the *izaar*, will be in the fire."[31]

Punishment is incurred either way regarding whatever hangs below the ankles. Nonetheless, if it is because of arrogance and self-conceit, the punishment will be greater: Allaah will not speak to this person on the Day of Resurrection, will not look at him, or purify him, and he will have painful torment. However, if it wasn't on account of self-conceit then he will be punished in Hell, Allaah forbid.

If one asks, "What is the Sunnah (regarding this issue)?" We should respond that the Sunnah is

---

[31] Al-Bukhari collected it in Kitaabul Libaas under the chapter **"whatever hangs below the ankles will be in the fire"** (5787).

that clothing is to be worn anywhere above the ankles to the middle of the shin; in the middle of the shin, or just below the middle of the shin, or what is just above the ankle. This is the Sunnah since this was the dress of the Prophet (*sallallahu 'alayhi wa sallam*) and his companions. The companions would not let their clothing exceed the ankles; it would be to the middle of the shin or slightly above the ankle. All of that is from the Sunnah, and Allaah is the One who grants success.

HADITH NUMBERS 617, 618, & 619

(٦) ١٧٦- عَنْ أَبِي هُرَيْرَةَ رَضِيَ اللهُ عَنْهُ قَالَ : قَالَ رَسُولُ

اللهِ صَلَّى اللهُ عَلَيْهِ وَ سَلَّمَ : ((ثَلَاثَةٌ لَا يُكَلِّمُهُمُ اللهُ

يَوْمَ الْقِيَامَةِ، وَ لَا يُزَكِّيهِمْ، وَ لَا يَنْظُرُ إِلَيْهِمْ، وَ لَهُمْ

عَذَابٌ أَلِيمٌ : شَيْخٌ زَانٍ، وَ مَلِكٌ كَذَّابٌ، وَ عَائِلٌ

مُسْتَكْبِرٌ)) رَوَاهُ مُسْلِمٌ .

6/617- On the authority of Aboo Hurairah (_radhiallahu 'anhu_), he said, "Allaah's Messenger (_sallallahu 'alayhi wa sallam_) said, "There are three people whom Allaah will not speak to, nor purify, nor look at on the day of resurrection, and they will have a painful torment. They are: an elderly person who fornicates, a lying ruler, and an arrogant, destitute person." Muslim collected it.[32]

---

[32] Muslim collected it in Kitaabul Emaan under the chapter **"Clarifying the mistake in prohibiting the dragging of the _izaar_"** (107).

(٧) ٦١٨ - وَ عَنْهُ رَضِيَ اللهُ عَنْهُ قَالَ : قَالَ رَسُولُ اللهِ صَلَّى اللهُ عَلَيْهِ وَ سَلَّمَ قَالَ : ((قَالَ اللهُ عَزَّ وَ جَلَّ : الْعِزُّ إِزَارِي ، وَ الْكِبْرِيَاءُ رِدَائِي ، فَمَنْ يُنَازِعُنِي عَذَّبْتُهُ)) رَوَاهُ مُسْلِمٌ .

7/618- On the authority of Aboo Hurairah (*radhiallahu 'anhu*), he said, "Allaah's Messenger (*sallallahu 'alayhi wa sallam*) said, "Allaah, the Mighty and Majestic said, "Might is My *izaar* and greatness is My cloak, so whoever contends with Me for either of them, I will punish him." Muslim collected it.[33]

(٨) ٦١٩ - وَ عَنْهُ رَضِيَ اللهُ عَنْهُ أَنَّ رَسُولَ اللهِ صَلَّى اللهُ عَلَيْهِ وَ سَلَّمَ قَالَ : ((بَيْنَمَا رَجُلٌ يَمْشِي فِي حُلَّةٍ تُعْجِبُهُ نَفْسُهُ ، مُرَجِّلٌ رَأْسَهُ ، يَخْتَالُ فِي مِشْيَتِهِ إِذْ خَسَفَ اللهُ بِهِ ، فَهُوَ يَتَجَلْجَلُ فِي الْأَرْضِ إِلَى يَوْمِ الْقِيَامَةِ)) مُتَّفَقٌ عَلَيْهِ .

---

[33] Muslim collected it in Kitaabul Birr wa Silah under the chapter **"Tahreem birr"** (2620).

((مُرَجَّلٌ رَأْسَهُ)) أَيْ : مُمَشَّطُهُ : ((يَتَجَلْجَلُ))

بِالْجِيمَيْنِ، أَيْ : يَغُوصُ وَ يَنْزِلُ .

8/619- On the authority of Aboo Hurairah (*radhiallahu 'anhu*), he said, "Once a man was walking with good clothes, being conceited, his hair groomed, boasting in his walking when suddenly Allaah caused the earth to swallow him; and he sank inside the earth and disappeared until the Day of Resurrection." (Agreed upon)[34]

Explanation

The author (*rahimahullah*) narrates these narrations in his book *Riyadh As-Saliheen* under the chapter "The prohibition of arrogance and self-conceit." He cited on the authority of Aboo Hurairah (*radhiallahu 'anhu*) that the Prophet (*sallallahu 'alayhi wa sallam*) said,

ثَلَاثَةٌ لَا يُكَلِّمُهُمُ اللهُ يَوْمَ الْقِيَامَةِ، وَ لَا

يُزَكِّيهِمْ، وَ لَا يَنْظُرُ إِلَيْهِمْ

---

[34] Al-Bukhari collected it in Kitaabul Libaas under the chapter **"Whoever drags his clothes is from the arrogant"** (5790); and Muslim collected it in Kitaabul Libaas wa Zinah under the chapter **"The prohibition of boasting in walking"** (2088).

"Three people whom Allaah will not speak to, nor purify, nor look at on the day of resurrection."

The meaning behind the word **"three"** is three types of people. What is not intended by it is "three men." The statement could be referring to thousands of people. Nevertheless, the intended meaning is "three types of people." When three, seven, or another number is mentioned, it counts the types of people not literally three individuals.

The first of them is,

شَـيْـخٌ زَانٍ

"an elderly person who fornicates."

Allaah will not speak to this person on the Day of Resurrection, nor look at him, or purify him; and he will have a painful torment.

The underlying reason behind such punishment for the elderly person is because his lust is no longer burning such that it would drive him to commit such an act. It is possible that the young person has a lust and is unable to control himself; nevertheless the old man's lust has become weakened, vanished, or has diminished greatly. So the fact that he is committing such act demonstrates how disgusting this person is, Allaah forbid, since he committed the act of fornication without a strong force that pushed him to it.

Fornication is an abomination whether from a young person or an elderly person; nonetheless, it's more repulsive and disgraceful when it is committed by an elderly person, Allaah forbid. This narration is restricted to what has been established in Al-Bukhari and Muslim that whoever commits such filthy acts and faced penalty in the *dunya*, Allaah will not combine two punishments (i.e. in the hereafter).[35] The penalty he underwent in the *dunya* would clear his record.

The second one is,

مَـلِكٌ كَـذَّابٌ

---

[35] Shaykh 'Uthaymeen is alluding to the hadith of 'Ubaada bin As-Saamit (radhiallahu 'anhu) he said, **"We were in the company of the Prophet (*sallallahu 'alayhi wa sallam*) in a sitting when he said, 'Whoever is afflicted by any of that and is punished it will be his atonement; and whoever is afflicted by that and Allaah conceals it if Allaah wills He will forgive him and if He wills He will punish him.'"** Al-Bukhari collected it in Kitaabul Al-Huduud under the chapter **"Punishment is atonement"** (6784); and Muslim collected it in Kitaabul Al-Huduud under the chapter **"Punishments are an atonement for those who committed it"** (1709).

"a lying ruler."

The word **"lying"** is an adjective that asserts an inseparable characteristic of the person described, which emphasizes that this person is a habitual liar. The ruler has no need to lie; his word imposes authority over the people. So he has no need to lie. When he begins lying, he promises the people; yet he does not fulfill it. For example, he says, "I will do such and such," yet he doesn't, or he says, "I will abandon such and such," yet he doesn't. He undermines the intelligence of the people and deceives them.

This individual, Allaah forbids, falls under this threat cited in the hadith. Allaah will not speak to him, or look at him, or purify him on the day of resurrection; and he will have a painful torment.

Lying is prohibited for the ruler and others; nonetheless, lies from a ruler are greater and more severe since he has no need to lie. So the ruler is obliged to be crystal clear. If he wants something, he should say, "Yes, I agree with it and I will do it." If he doesn't want it he should say, "I do not agree (with it) and I will not do it." An ordinary person may feel the need to lie (because he feels powerless otherwise) and do so, but the ruler does not need to.

Lying is prohibited and among the traits of the hypocrites, Allaah forbid. Indeed, whenever a hypocrite speaks, he lies and it is impermissible for anyone to lie unrestrictedly. Some laymen say, "Lying is harmless as long as it doesn't cause unpleasant consequences." This is a satanic principle, totally groundless and religiously baseless. The correct (position) is lying is unlawful in every situation.

The third individual is,

"a destitute arrogant person"

this is the focus of our discussion on this hadith. The word **"destitute"** refers to being poor; and the word **"arrogant"** refers to one who belittles people, Allaah forbid. The poor person does not possess what causes arrogance. Perhaps the rich person's wealth could alter him and cause him to desire falsehood. Consequentially he is arrogant toward Allaah's servants and the truth. But the poor man does not have two nickels to rub together. So in this state, how can he be arrogant?

Therefore, Allaah will not speak to the destitute, arrogant person on the day of resurrection, nor look at him, or purify him; and he will have a painful torment.

Arrogance is prohibited for the wealthy as well as the destitute, yet arrogance in the destitute is more repulsive. Because of this when people see a wealthy person being humble they deem it strange and great, and they consider this wealthy person to possess the noblest qualities. Yet if they found a poor humble person then he is like the rest of the people since poverty necessitates that person be humble.

So if a person who is destitute and poor, Allaah forbid, begins being arrogant to the creation or rejects the truth, then He has no motive to be arrogant and thereby falls under the category highlighted in this hadith.

Afterwards, the author *(rahimahullah)* mentions what has been narrated of evidences for the prohibition of arrogance and self-conceit, which are among the major sins. On the authority of Aboo Hurairah *(radhiallahu 'anhu)*, the Prophet *(sallallahu 'alayhi wa sallam)* said,

الْـعِزُّ إِزَارِي ، وَ الْكِبْـرِيَاءُ رِدَائِي ، فَـمَـنْ يُنَازِعُـنِي عَـذَّبْـتُـهُ

"Might is My *izaar* and greatness is My cloak, so whoever contends with Me for either of them, I will punish him."[36]

This (hadith) is among the *Qudsi* narrations, which the Prophet (*sallallahu 'alayhi wa sallam*) narrated from Allaah; and they are not on the level of the Qur'ân. The Qur'ân has certain rulings specific to it. Among them is a miracle, which mankind cannot produce the likes of, or ten chapters, or even a single chapter or anything similar to it. It is impermissible for one who has a major sexual impurity to read the Qur'ân; and the prayer is only valid if he reads the Qur'ân—rather he is obliged to recite surah Fatihah. *Qudsi* narrations do not have these attributes.

The Qur'ân is preserved; nothing is added or taken away, or transmitted in meaning; all of it is authentically narrated. As for the *Qudsi* narrations, they are narrated in meaning; lots of them are weak and fabricated. What is important is the *Qudsi* narrations are not on the same level as the Qur'ân except that it is stated that the Prophet (*sallallahu 'alayhi wa sallam*) narrated it from his Lord.

Allaah, the Sublime says,

---

[36] Muslim collected it in Kitaabul Birr wa Silah under the chapter **"prohibition of arrogance"** (2620).

الْـعِـزُّ إِزَارِي ، وَ الْـكِـبْـرِيَـاءُ رِدَائِـي

"Might is My *izaar* and greatness is My cloak."

This hadith is among the narrations, which should be treated literally and any attempt to alter or interpret it metaphorically is unacceptable; instead it is only stated in the manner Allaah, the Sublime says that was narrated by the Prophet (*sallallahu 'alayhi sallam*). Whoever disputes Allaah's might and wants to take power similar to Allaah's power, or whoever disputes over Allaah's greatness and is arrogant to Allaah's servants, Allaah will punish him.

Then the author cited the last hadith of Aboo Hurairah from the Prophet (*sallallahu 'alayhi wa sallam*) in which he said,

بَـيْـنَـمَـا رَجُـلٌ يَـمْـشِـي فِـي حُـلَّـةٍ تُـعْـجِـبُـهُ نَـفْـسُـهُ ،

مُـرَجِّـلٌ رَأْسَـهُ ، يَـخْـتَـالُ فِـي مِـشْـيَـتِـهِ

"Once a man was walking with good clothes, being conceited, his hair groomed, boasting in his walking,"

Meaning, he had an air of conceitedness, arrogance, and haughtiness.

إِذْ خَسَفَ اللهُ بِهِ

"When suddenly Allaah caused the earth to swallow him,"

Meaning, Allaah made the ground swallow him.

فَهُوَ يَتَجَلْجَلُ فِي الْأَرْضِ إِلَى يَوْمِ الْقِيَامَةِ

"And he sank into the earth and disappeared until the Day of Resurrection."

Meaning, the earth closed over him, he sank into it, and was buried.

فَهُوَ يَتَجَلْجَلُ فِي الْأَرْضِ إِلَى يَوْمِ الْقِيَامَةِ

"and disappeared until the day of resurrection."

This is similar to Qaaroon, whom the author (*rahimahullah*) cited in the beginning of this chapter. Qaaroon came out to his people in his pomp.

﴿ فَخَرَجَ عَلَىٰ قَوْمِهِۦ فِى زِينَتِهِۦ قَالَ ٱلَّذِينَ يُرِيدُونَ ٱلْحَيَوٰةَ ٱلدُّنْيَا يَٰلَيْتَ لَنَا مِثْلَ مَآ أُوتِىَ قَٰرُونُ إِنَّهُۥ لَذُو حَظٍّ عَظِيمٍ ۝ وَقَالَ ٱلَّذِينَ أُوتُوا۟ ٱلْعِلْمَ وَيْلَكُمْ ثَوَابُ ٱللَّهِ خَيْرٌ لِّمَنْ ءَامَنَ وَعَمِلَ

صَٰلِحًا وَلَا يُلَقَّىٰهَآ إِلَّا ٱلصَّٰبِرُونَ ۝ فَخَسَفْنَا بِهِۦ وَبِدَارِهِ ٱلْأَرْضَ

فَمَا كَانَ لَهُۥ مِن فِئَةٍ يَنصُرُونَهُۥ مِن دُونِ ٱللَّهِ وَمَا كَانَ مِنَ

ٱلْمُنتَصِرِينَ ۝

"Those who were desirous of the life of the world, said: "Ah, would that we had the like of what Qaaroon has been given. Verily! He is the owner of a great fortune." But those who had been given (religious) knowledge said: "Woe to you! The Reward of Allaah (in the Hereafter) is better for those who believe and do righteous good deeds, and this none shall attain except those who are patient (in following the truth)." So We caused the earth to swallow him and his dwelling place. Then he had no group or party to help him against Allaah, nor was he one of those who could save themselves."[37]

The statement, **"and he sank into the earth"** maybe that the person sank into the earth but he is still alive and will remain as he is until the Day of Judgment, suffering, and will receive the

---

[37] Al-Qasas (28:79-81)

same torment in the grave, but the manner of such torment is not known to us.

In this hadith, the aforementioned narrations as well as what comes after prove the prohibition of arrogance and self-conceit; and that the person is obliged to observe his status and place himself in his rightful position, and Allaah is the One who grants success.

HADITH NUMBER 620

(٩) - ٦٢٠ - وَ عَنْ سَلَمَةَ بْنِ الْأَكْوَعِ رَضِيَ اللهُ عَنْهُ قَالَ :
قَالَ رَسُولُ اللهِ صَلَّى اللهُ عَلَيْهِ وَ سَلَّمَ : ((لَا يَزَالُ
الرَّجُلُ يَذْهَبُ بِنَفْسِهِ حَتَّى يُكْتَبَ فِي الْجَبَّارِينَ ،
فَيُصِيبَهُ مَا أَصَابَهُمْ)) رَوَاهُ التِّرْمَذِي وَ قَالَ : حَدِيثٌ
حَسَنٌ .

((يَذْهَبُ بِنَفْسِهِ)) أَيْ : يَرْتَفِعُ وَ يَتَكَبَّرُ

9/620- On the authority of Salamah bin Al-Akwaa' (*radhiallahu 'anhu*), he said, 'Allaah's Messenger (*sallallahu 'alayhi wa sallam*) said, "The man remains elevating himself until he is written down among the tyrannical, so he suffers what they (the tyrannical) have suffered." At-Tirmidhī collected it.[38]

---

[38] At-Tirmidhī collected it in the Kitaabul Birr wa Silah under the chapter **"What is mentioned regarding**

The phrase **'elevating himself'** refers to deeming himself above others and being arrogant.

Explanation

In the last hadith of this chapter, the Prophet (*sallallahu 'alayhi wa sallam*) warns the person from self-conceit. The horrific punishment designated for the tyrants mentioned in the following verse is sufficient for a warning,

"Thus does Allaah seal up the heart of every arrogant tyrant. (So they cannot guide themselves to the Right Path)."[39]

The tyrant's heart, Allaah forbid, is sealed up from any good reaching it while the heart is not impeded from committing evil.

In summary, this chapter revolves around two matters:

1. The prohibition of arrogance, which is among the major sins.

---

arrogance" (2000); and he said, "this hadith is Hasan Ghareeb (i.e., what occurs in the text of the hadith of obscure wording remote from being understood due to the lack of its usage).

[39] Ghafir (40:35)

2. The prohibition of self-conceit, which is also among the unlawful matters. This act may render deeds fruitless when one becomes conceited about his worship or his recitation of the Qur'ân and so forth. Perhaps his reward is nullified while he is unaware of it.

NOTES

Printed in Great Britain
by Amazon

66718278R00040